All
Mixed
Up

A Collection of Limericks for Kids

Written by Brent Aronsen
Illustrated by Claire Okkema

ISBN: 1494414708
ISBN 13: 9781494414702

Library of Congress Control Number: 2013922531
CreateSpace Independent Publishing Platform, North Charleston, SC

To everyone
who believes in our dreams

All Mixed Up

She thought a smile was a frown
And the sky was the ground.
But, in her defense,
It all made sense
'Cause she was hanging upside down.

Imaginary Friend

Go on and extend
Your hand to my friend.
Make no mistake.
He'll give it a shake,
Even if he is pretend.

Not This Time

You may not think she's cool,
But your mother is no fool.
For goodness' sake,
Your cough is fake,
So get up and go to school!

Soccer Star

My grandma got off her rocker
And joined us in some soccer.
She stole the ball
And schooled us all.
Boy, was that a shocker!

A New Outfit

She wore a nice skirt
That matched her white shirt.
But, as she played on the ground,
She quickly found
She now wore lots of dirt.

The Dream

The little boy had learned to fly
Above the clouds, way up high.
He had so much fun,
Until he was done,
When he woke up with a sigh.

A Bold Prediction

Tell me that you'll bake
A big chocolate cake.
I'll stand up tall
And eat it all,
And my tummy will not ache!

Tough Sister

Colliding on the slide,
The twins fell off the side.
He scraped his knee,
And so did she,
But it was only he who cried.

Bedhead

He must have rolled around
'Cause in the morning he found
Every hair on his head
That he'd combed before bed
Was no longer staying down!

Leftovers

I know you tried to tell me
That they were rather smelly.
Judging by the mold,
They were really old,
But now they're in my belly!

Sticky Eater

As an eater, he is picky,
So feeding him is tricky.
Too runny, too lumpy,
Too funny, too bumpy,
But never is it too sticky!

My Pet Porcupine

My porcupine once nearly
Poked my spine severely.
So if it runs away,
I don't think I'll say,
"I miss it very dearly."

Holy Cow!

A cow has mastered flight?
What a crazy sight!
Oh, never mind.
Perhaps I'm blind.
That cow is just a kite.

Zoo: Part 1

What would you do
If, out of the blue,
Led by an ape,
There was an escape
At your local zoo?

Zoo: Part II

Take an elephant for a spin
Or grab a shark by its fin?
Running around town
To chase a tiger down,
You'd surely fit right in!

Allowance Negotiation

I know you are amazed
I've made my bed for days.
What I'm trying to say
Is if you want this to stay,
I demand a raise!

Hyper

I bop, and I flop,
And I just can't stop.
Up I'm wound
From having downed
Three whole cans of pop!

Dentist Appointment

You are telling me to scurry,
That we really have to hurry.
But if we're late or whether
We miss it altogether,
It won't cause *me* much worry.

Punishment

I see it over there—
The corner with the chair.
I'll go do my time
For committing the crime
Of cutting my sister's hair.

No More Chores!

Whether we're in Maine or Minnesota,
It matters not an iota.
So, parents, before
You give us a chore,
Know we've already reached our quota.

A Forced Admission

Since I'm under duress,
I suppose I'll confess
'Cause that's the only way
You'll get me to say,
"My room is kind of a mess."

Brain Strain

Sometimes I try to refrain
From having to use my brain
'Cause my brain is such
That if I think too much,
I'm sure to give it a strain.

Not Possible

To deal with my confusion,
I've come to this conclusion:
That planes can fly
Up in the sky
Is merely an illusion.

For Those Who Love to Read

Under my blankets at night,
I turn on my secret light.
I read as I please,
My mind is at ease,
And all in the world is right.

For Those Who Don't

When you stopped to say, "Hey,"
I thought we would play.
But I took one look,
Saw your big book,
And quickly ran away.

Presents

If you give your presents a shake,
You should learn from my mistake.
HANDLE WITH CARE
Means you better beware:
Shaking can make them break!

Pursue Your Passion

Whether it's music, sports, or fashion,
Continue to pursue your passion.
And when you make it very far,
Be thankful for where you are,
And always show compassion.

33292537R00020